P9-ASN-564

WITHDRAWN

THE CONGO
AND OTHER POEMS

BY

VACHEL LINDSAY

WITH AN INTRODUCTION BY

HARRIET MONROE

EDITOR OF "POETRY"

New York

THE MACMILLAN COMPANY

1915

All rights reserved

Copyright, 1913, by Harriet Monroe and by the *Independent*.
Copyright, 1914, by Harriet Monroe, by Margaret C. Anderson, the *Little Review*, by the *Metropolitan*, and by the Phillips Publishing Company.

———

COPYRIGHT, 1914,

BY THE MACMILLAN COMPANY.

———

Set up and electrotyped.   Published September, 1914.
Reprinted March, 1915.

PS
3523
I58
C6
1914

Norwood Press
J. S. Cushing Co. — Berwick & Smith Co.
Norwood, Mass., U.S.A.

" I respectfully submit these poems as experiments in which I endeavor to carry this vaudeville form back towards the old Greek precedent of the half-chanted lyric. In this case the one-third of music must be added by the instinct of the reader. He must be Iophon. And he can easily be Iophon if he brings to bear upon the piece what might be called the Higher Vaudeville imagination. . . .

" Big general contrasts between the main sections should be the rule of the first attempts at improvising. It is the hope of the writer that after two or three readings each line will suggest its own separate touch of melody to the reader who has become accustomed to the cadences. Let him read what he likes read, and sing what he likes sung."

It was during this same visit in Chicago, at *Poetry's* banquet on the evening of March first, 1914, that Mr. Yeats honored Mr. Lindsay by addressing his after-dinner talk primarily to him as " a fellow craftsman," and by saying of *General Booth*:

" This poem is stripped bare of ornament; it has an earnest simplicity, a strange beauty, and you know Bacon said, ' There is no excellent beauty without strangeness.' "

This recognition from the distinguished Irish poet tempts me to hint at the cosmopolitan aspects of such racily local art as Mr. Lindsay's. The subject is too large for a merely introductory word, but the reader may be invited to reflect upon it. If Mr. Lindsay's poetry should cross the ocean, it would not be the first time that our most indigenous art has reacted upon the art of older nations. Besides Poe — who, though indigenous in ways too subtle for brief analysis, yet passed all frontiers in his swift, sad flight — the two American artists of widest influence, Whitman and Whistler, have been intensely American in temperament and in the special spiritual quality of their art.

If Whistler was the first great artist to accept the modern message in Oriental art, if Whitman was the first great modern poet to discard the limitations of conventional form: if both were more free, more individual, than their contemporaries, this was the expression of their Americanism, which may perhaps be defined as a spiritual independence and love of adventure inherited from the pioneers. Foreign artists are usually the first to recognize this new tang; one detects the influence of the great dead poet and dead painter in all modern art which looks forward instead of back; and their countrymen, our own contemporary poets and painters, often express indirectly, through French influences, a reaction which they are reluctant to confess directly.

A lighter phase of this foreign enthusiasm for the American tang is confessed by Signor Marinetti, the Italian "futurist," when in his article on *Futurism and the Theatre*, in *The Mask*, he urges the revolutionary value of "American eccentrics," citing the fundamental primitive quality in their vaudeville art. This may be another statement of Mr. Lindsay's plea for a closer relation between the poet and his audience, for a return

to the healthier open-air conditions, and immediate per-
sonal contacts, in the art of the Greeks and of primitive nations. Such conditions and contacts may still
be found, if the world only knew it, in the wonderful
song-dances of the Hopis and others of our aboriginal
tribes. They may be found, also, in a measure, in the
quick response between artist and audience in modern
vaudeville. They are destined to a wider and higher
influence; in fact, the development of that influence, the
return to primitive sympathies between artist and audience, which may make possible once more the assertion
of primitive creative power, is recognized as the immediate movement in modern art. It is a movement
strong enough to persist in spite of extravagances and
absurdities; strong enough, it may be hoped, to fulfil its
purpose and revitalize the world.

It is because Mr. Lindsay's poetry seems to be defi-
nitely in that movement that it is, I think, important.

HARRIET MONROE.

TABLE OF CONTENTS

xi

THIRD SECTION

A Miscellany called the Christmas Tree

Rhymes for Gloriana

FOURTH SECTION

Twenty Moon Poems

First Section

Moon Poems for the Children

Second Section

The Moon is a Mirror

TABLE OF CONTENTS

For permission to reprint some of the poems contained in this volume the author is indebted to the courtesy of the editors and publishers of the *Metropolitan*, *Poetry: A Magazine of Verse*, the *Independent*, *Tuck's Magazine*, *Reedy's Mirror*, the *Little Review*, and the *American Magazine*.

FIRST SECTION

Poems intended to be read aloud, or chanted.

THE CONGO

A STUDY OF THE NEGRO RACE

I. Their Basic Savagery

Fat black bucks in a wine-barrel room,

Barrel-house kings, with feet unstable,

Sagged and reeled and pounded on the table, *A deep rolling bass.*

Pounded on the table,

Beat an empty barrel with the handle of a broom,

Hard as they were able,

Boom, boom, Boom,

With a silk umbrella and the handle of a broom,

Boomlay, boomlay, boomlay, Boom.

Then I had religion, Then I had a vision.

I could not turn from their revel in derision.

Then I saw the Congo, creeping through the black, *More deliberate. Solemnly chanted.*

3

C<small>UTTING</small> <small>THROUGH THE FOREST WITH A</small>
  <small>GOLDEN TRACK.</small>

Then along that riverbank
A thousand miles
Tattooed cannibals danced in files ;
Then I heard the boom of the blood-lust
  song
And a thigh-bone beating on a tin-pan gong. *A rapidly*
And "B<small>LOOD</small>" screamed the whistles and *piling climax*
  the fifes of the warriors, *of speed and*
racket.
"B<small>LOOD</small>" screamed the skull-faced, lean
  witch-doctors,
" Whirl ye the deadly voo-doo rattle,
Harry the uplands,
Steal all the cattle,
Rattle-rattle, rattle-rattle,
Bing.
Boomlay, boomlay, boomlay, B<small>OOM</small>,"
A roaring, epic, rag-time tune *With a philo-*
From the mouth of the Congo *sophic pause.*
To the Mountains of the Moon.
Death is an Elephant,
Torch-eyed and horrible, *Shrilly and with*
a heavily ac-
Foam-flanked and terrible. *cented metre.*
B<small>OOM</small>, steal the pygmies,

Boom, kill the Arabs,
Boom, kill the white men,
Hoo, Hoo, Hoo.
Listen to the yell of Leopold's ghost   *Like the wind*
Burning in Hell for his hand-maimed host.   *in the chimney.*
Hear how the demons chuckle and yell
Cutting his hands off, down in Hell.
Listen to the creepy proclamation,
Blown through the lairs of the forest-nation,
Blown past the white-ants' hill of clay,
Blown past the marsh where the butter-
    flies play : —
"Be careful what you do,
Or Mumbo-Jumbo, God of the Congo,   *All the o sounds*
And all of the other   *very golden.*
Gods of the Congo,   *Heavy accents*
                                             very heavy.
                                             Light accents
Mumbo-Jumbo will hoo-doo you,   *very light. Last*
Mumbo-Jumbo will hoo-doo you,   *line whispered.*
Mumbo-Jumbo will hoo-doo you."

II. Their Irrepressible High Spirits

Wild crap-shooters with a whoop and a call   *Rather shrill*
Danced the juba in their gambling-hall   *and high.*
And laughed fit to kill, and shook the town,

And guyed the policemen and laughed them
    down
With a boomlay, boomlay, boomlay, BOOM.
THEN I SAW THE CONGO, CREEPING THROUGH   *Read exactly as*
    THE BLACK,   *in first section.*
CUTTING THROUGH THE FOREST WITH A
    GOLDEN TRACK.
A negro fairyland swung into view,   *Lay emphasis*
A minstrel river   *on the delicate*
Where dreams come true.   *ideas. Keep as*
                                     light-footed as
The ebony palace soared on high   *possible.*
Through the blossoming trees to the even-
    ing sky.
The inlaid porches and casements shone
With gold and ivory and elephant-bone.
And the black crowd laughed till their
    sides were sore
At the baboon butler in the agate door,
And the well-known tunes of the parrot
    band
That trilled on the bushes of that magic land.

A troupe of skull-faced witch-men came   *With pomposity.*
Through the agate doorway in suits of
    flame,

Yea, long-tailed coats with a gold-leaf crust
And hats that were covered with diamond-
dust.
And the crowd in the court gave a whoop
and a call
And,danced the juba from wall to wall.
But the witch-men suddenly stilled the
throng

With a great deliberation and ghostliness.

With a stern cold glare, and a stern old
song : —
"Mumbo-Jumbo will hoo-doo you." . . .
Just then from the doorway, as fat as
shotes,

With overwhelming assurance, good cheer, and pomp.

Came the cake-walk princes in their long
red coats,
Canes with a brilliant lacquer shine,
And tall silk hats that were red as wine.
And they pranced with their butterfly
partners there,

With growing speed and sharply marked dance-rhythm.

Coal-black maidens with pearls in their
hair,
Knee-skirts trimmed with the jassamine
sweet,
And bells on their ankles and little black-
feet.

And the couples railed at the chant and
    the frown
Of the witch-men lean, and laughed them
    down.
(O rare was the revel, and well worth while
That made those glowering witch-men smile.)

The cake-walk royalty then began
To walk for a cake that was tall as a man
To the tune of "Boomlay, boomlay, Boom,"
While the witch-men laughed, with a sinis-   *With a touch of*
    ter air,   *negro dialect,*
                                              and
And sang with the scalawags prancing   *as rapidly as*
    there : —   *possible toward*
                                              the end.
" Walk with care, walk with care,
Or Mumbo-Jumbo, God of the Congo,
And all of the other
Gods of the Congo,
Mumbo-Jumbo will hoo-doo you.
Beware, beware, walk with care,
Boomlay, boomlay, boomlay, boom.
Boomlay, boomlay, boomlay, boom,
Boomlay, boomlay, boomlay, boom,
Boomlay, boomlay, boomlay,
Boom."

Oh rare was the revel, and well worth while
That made those glowering witch-men smile.

Slow philo-sophic calm.

III. THE HOPE OF THEIR RELIGION

A good old negro in the slums of the town
Preached at a sister for her velvet gown.
Howled at a brother for his low-down ways,
His prowling, guzzling, sneak-thief days.
Beat on the Bible till he wore it out
Starting the jubilee revival shout.
And some had visions, as they stood on
  chairs,
And sang of Jacob, and the golden stairs,
And they all repented, a thousand strong
From their stupor and savagery and sin and
  wrong
And slammed with their hymn books till
  they shook the room
With "glory, glory, glory,"
And "Boom, boom, BOOM."
THEN I SAW THE CONGO, CREEPING THROUGH
  THE BLACK
CUTTING THROUGH THE JUNGLE WITH A
  GOLDEN TRACK.

*Heavy bass.
With a literal
imitation of
camp-meeting
racket, and
trance.*

*Exactly as in
the first section.
Begin with
terror and
power, end with
joy.*

And the gray sky opened like a new-rent
    veil

And showed the apostles with their coats of
    mail.

In bright white steele they were seated
    round

And their fire-eyes watched where the Congo
    wound.

And the twelve Apostles, from their thrones
    on high

Thrilled all the forest with their heavenly
    cry : —

"Mumbo-Jumbo will die in the jungle;

Never again will he hoo-doo you,

Never again will he hoo-doo you."

Sung to the tune of "Hark, ten thousand harps and voices."

Then along that river, a thousand miles

The vine-snared trees fell down in files.

Pioneer angels cleared the way

For a Congo paradise, for babes at play,

For sacred capitals, for temples clean.

Gone were the skull-faced witch-men lean.

There, where the wild ghost-gods had wailed

A million boats of the angels sailed

With oars of silver, and prows of blue

With growing deliberation and joy.

In a rather high key — as delicately as possible.

And silken pennants that the sun shone
    through.
'Twas a land transfigured, 'twas a new
    creation.
Oh, a singing wind swept the negro nation
And on through the backwoods clearing
    flew : —
"Mumbo-Jumbo is dead in the jungle.   *To the tune of*
Never again will he hoo-doo you.   *"Hark, ten*
Never again will he hoo-doo you.   *thousand harps*
                                     and voices."

Redeemed were the forests, the beasts and
    the men,
And only the vulture dared again
By the far, lone mountains of the moon
To cry, in the silence, the Congo tune : —
Mumbo-Jumbo will hoo-doo you,   *Dying down*
" Mumbo-Jumbo will hoo-doo you.   *into a pene-*
Mumbo . . . Jumbo . . . will . . . hoo-doo . . .   *trating,*
    you."   *terrified*
                                     whisper.

THE SANTA–FE TRAIL. (A HUMORESQUE)

I asked the old Negro, "What is that bird that sings
so well?" He answered: "That is the Rachel-Jane."
"Hasn't it another name, lark, or thrush, or the like?"
"No. Jus' Rachel-Jane."

I. IN WHICH A RACING AUTO COMES FROM THE EAST

This is the order of the music of the morn-
    ing:—
First, from the far East comes but a croon-
    ing.
The crooning turns to a sunrise singing.
Hark to the *calm*-horn, *balm*-horn, *psalm*-
    horn.
Hark to the *faint*-horn, *quaint*-horn, *saint*-
    horn. . . .

*To be sung
delicately, to an
improvised
tune.*

Hark to the *pace*-horn, *chase*-horn, *race*-horn.
And the holy veil of the dawn has gone.
Swiftly the brazen car comes on.
It burns in the East as the sunrise burns.
I see great flashes where the far trail turns.

*To be sung or
read with great
speed.*

Its eyes are lamps like the eyes of dragons.

It drinks gasoline from big red flagons.

Butting through the delicate mists of the
 morning,

It comes like lightning, goes past roaring.

It will hail all the wind-mills, taunting,
 ringing,

Dodge the cyclones,

Count the milestones,

On through the ranges the prairie-dog tills —

Scooting past the cattle on the thousand
 hills. . . .

Ho for the tear-horn, scare-horn, dare-horn, *To be read or*

Ho for the *gay*-horn, *bark*-horn, *bay*-horn. *sung in a rolling*

bass, with some

Ho for Kansas, land that restores us *deliberation.*

When houses choke us, and great books bore us!

Sunrise Kansas, harvester's Kansas,

A million men have found you before us.

II. IN WHICH MANY AUTOS PASS WESTWARD

I want live things in their pride to remain. *In an even,*

deliberate,

I will not kill one grasshopper vain *narrative*

Though he eats a hole in my shirt like a *manner.*
 door.

I let him out, give him one chance more.

Perhaps, while he gnaws my hat in his whim,

Grasshopper lyrics occur to him.

I am a tramp by the long trail's border,

Given to squalor, rags and disorder.

I nap and amble and yawn and look,

Write fool-thoughts in my grubby book,

Recite to the children, explore at my ease,

Work when I work, beg when I please,

Give crank-drawings, that make folks stare

To the half-grown boys in the sunset glare,

And get me a place to sleep in the hay

At the end of a live-and-let-live day.

I find in the stubble of the new-cut weeds

A whisper and a feasting, all one needs:

The whisper of the strawberries, white and
     red

Here where the new-cut weeds lie dead.

But I would not walk all alone till I die

Without some life-drunk horns going by.

Up round this apple-earth they come

Blasting the whispers of the morning
     dumb: —

Cars in a plain realistic row.
And fair dreams fade
When the raw horns blow.

On each snapping pennant
A big black name: —
The careering city
Whence each car came.
They tour from Memphis, Atlanta, Savannah,
Tallahassee and Texarkana.
They tour from St. Louis, Columbus,
    Manistee,
They tour from Peoria, Davenport, Kan-
    kakee.
Cars from Concord, Niagara, Boston,
Cars from Topeka, Emporia, and Austin.
Cars from Chicago, Hannibal, Cairo.
Cars from Alton, Oswego, Toledo.
Cars from Buffalo, Kokomo, Delphi,
Cars fom Lodi, Carmi, Loami.
Ho for Kansas, land that restores us
When houses choke us, and great books bore
    us !
While I watch the highroad
And look at the sky,

*Like a train-
caller in a
Union Depot.*

While I watch the clouds in amazing
    grandeur
Roll their legions without rain
Over the blistering Kansas plain —
While I sit by the milestone
And watch the sky,
The United States
Goes by.

Listen to the iron-horns, ripping, racking.

Listen to the quack-horns, slack and clack-
    ing.

Way down the road, trilling like a toad,

Here comes the *dice*-horn, here comes the
    vice-horn,

Here comes the *snarl*-horn, *brawl*-horn, *lewd*-
    horn,

Followed by the *prude*-horn, bleak and
    squeaking : —

(Some of them from Kansas, some of them
    from Kansas.)

Here comes the *hod*-horn, *plod*-horn, *sod*-
    horn,

Nevermore-to-*roam*-horn, *loam*-horn, *home*-
    horn.

*To be given
very harshly,
with a
snapping ex-
plosiveness.*

(Some of them from Kansas, some of them
    from Kansas.)

    Far away the Rachel-Jane *To be read or*
    Not defeated by the horns *sung, well-nigh*
    Sings amid a hedge of thorns : — *in a whisper.*
    "Love and life,
    Eternal youth —
    Sweet, sweet, sweet, sweet,
    Dew and glory,
    Love and truth,
    Sweet, sweet, sweet, sweet."

WHILE SMOKE-BLACK FREIGHTS ON THE *Louder and*
    DOUBLE-TRACKED RAILROAD, *louder, faster*
and faster.

DRIVEN AS THOUGH BY THE FOUL-FIEND'S
    OX-GOAD,

SCREAMING TO THE WEST COAST, SCREAM-
    ING TO THE EAST,

CARRY OFF A HARVEST, BRING BACK A
    FEAST,

HARVESTING MACHINERY AND HARNESS FOR
    THE BEAST.

THE HAND-CARS WHIZ, AND RATTLE ON THE
    RAILS,

THE SUNLIGHT FLASHES ON THE TIN
    DINNER-PAILS.

    C

And then, in an instant,

Ye modern men,

Behold the procession once again,

Listen to the iron-horns, ripping, racking,

Listen to the *wise*-horn, desperate-to-*advise* horn,

Listen to the *fast*-horn, *kill*-horn, *blast*-horn. . . .

> Far away the Rachel-Jane
>
> Not defeated by the horns
>
> Sings amid a hedge of thorns : —
>
> Love and life,
>
> Eternal youth,
>
> Sweet, sweet, sweet, sweet,
>
> Dew and glory,
>
> Love and truth.
>
> Sweet, sweet, sweet, sweet.

The mufflers open on a score of cars

With wonderful thunder,

CRACK, CRACK, CRACK,

CRACK-CRACK, CRACK-CRACK,

CRACK-CRACK-CRACK, . . .

Listen to the gold-horn . . .

Old-horn . . .

Cold-horn . . .

In a rolling bass, with increasing deliberation.

With a snapping explosiveness.

To be sung or read well-nigh in a whisper.

To be brawled in the beginning with a snapping explosiveness, ending in a languorous chant.

And all of the tunes, till the night comes
    down

On hay-stack, and ant-hill, and wind-bitten
    town.

Then far in the west, as in the beginning,

Dim in the distance, sweet in retreating,

Hark to the faint-horn, quaint-horn, saint-
    horn,

Hark to the calm-horn, balm-horn, psalm-
    horn. . . .

*To be sung to
exactly the
same whispered
tune as the first
five lines.*

They are hunting the goals that they under-
    stand : —

San-Francisco and the brown sea-sand.

My goal is the mystery the beggars win.

I am caught in the web the night-winds
    spin.

The edge of the wheat-ridge speaks to me.

I talk with the leaves of the mulberry tree.

And now I hear, as I sit all alone

In the dusk, by another big Santa-Fe stone,

The souls of the tall corn gathering round

And the gay little souls of the grass in the
    ground.

Listen to the tale the cotton-wood tells.

*This section
beginning
sonorously,
ending in a
languorous
whisper.*

Listen to the wind-mills, singing o'er the
    wells.
Listen to the whistling flutes without price
Of myriad prophets out of paradise.
Harken to the wonder
That the night-air carries. . . .
Listen . . . to . . . the . . . whisper . . .
Of . . . the . . . prairie . . . fairies
    Singing o'er the fairy plain : —
    "Sweet, sweet, sweet, sweet.
    Love and glory,
    Stars and rain,
    Sweet, sweet, sweet, sweet. . . ."

To the same whispered tune as the Rachel-Jane song — but very slowly.

THE FIREMEN'S BALL

Section One

"Give the engines room,
Give the engines room."
Louder, faster
The little band-master
Whips up the fluting,
Hurries up the tooting.
He thinks that he stands,
The reins in his hands,
In the fire-chief's place
In the night alarm chase.
The cymbals whang,
The kettledrums bang: —
"Clear the street,
Clear the street,
Clear the street — Boom, boom.
In the evening gloom,
In the evening gloom,
Give the engines room,
Give the engines room,

To be read, or chanted, with the heavy buzzing bass of fire-engines pumping.

In this passage the reading or chanting is shriller and higher.

Lest souls be trapped
In a terrible tomb."
The sparks and the pine-brands
Whirl on high
From the black and reeking alleys
To the wide red sky.
Hear the hot glass crashing,
Hear the stone steps hissing.
Coal black streams
Down the gutters pour.
There are cries for help
From a far fifth floor.
For a longer ladder
Hear the fire-chief call.
Listen to the music
Of the firemen's ball.
Listen to the music
Of the firemen's ball.
" 'Tis the
NIGHT
Of doom,"
Say the ding-dong doom-bells.
" NIGHT
Of doom,"
Say the ding-dong doom-bells.

*To be read
or chanted in
a heavy bass.*

Faster, faster
The red flames come.
"Hum grum," say the engines,
"Hum grum grum."
"Buzz, buzz,"

Shriller and higher.

Says the crowd.
"See, see,"
Calls the crowd.
"Look out,"
Yelps the crowd
And the high walls fall: —
Listen to the music
Of the firemen's ball.
Listen to the music
Of the firemen's ball.
"'Tis the

Heavy bass.

NIGHT
Of doom,"
Say the ding-dong doom-bells.
NIGHT
Of doom,
Say the ding-dong doom-bells.
Whangaranga, whangaranga,
Whang, whang, whang,
Clang, clang, clangaranga,

Clang, clang, clang.

Clang—a—ranga—

Clang—a—ranga—

Clang,

Clang,

Clang.

Listen — to — the — music —

Of the firemen's ball —

Bass, much slower.

SECTION TWO

" Many's the heart that's breaking

If we could read them all

After the ball is over."   (An old song.)

Scornfully, gaily

The bandmaster sways,

Changing the strain

That the wild band plays.

With a red and royal intoxication,

A tangle of sounds

And a syncopation,

Sweeping and bending

From side to side,

Master of dreams,

With a peacock pride.

A lord of the delicate flowers of delight

To be read or sung slowly and softly, in the manner of lustful, insinuating music.

He drives compunction
Back through the night.
Dreams he's a soldier
Plumed and spurred,
And valiant lads
Arise at his word,
Flaying the sober
Thoughts he hates,
Driving them back
From the dream-town gates.
How can the languorous
Dancers know
The red dreams come
When the good dreams go?
"'Tis the
NIGHT
Of love,"
Call the silver joy-bells,
" NIGHT
Of love,"
Call the silver joy-bells.
"Honey and wine,
Honey and wine.
Sing low, now, violins,
Sing, sing low,

*To be read
or chanted
slowly and
softly in the
manner of
lustful insinu-
ating music.*

Blow gently, wood-wind,
Mellow and slow.
Like midnight poppies
The sweethearts bloom.
Their eyes flash power,
Their lips are dumb.
Faster and faster
Their pulses come,
Though softer now
The drum-beats fall.
Honey and wine,
Honey and wine.
'Tis the firemen's ball,
'Tis the firemen's ball.

"I am slain,"   *With a climax*
Cries true-love   *of whispered*
There in the shadow.   *mourning.*
"And I die,"
Cries true-love,
There laid low.
"When the fire-dreams come,
The wise dreams go."
BUT HIS CRY IS DROWNED   *Suddenly in-*
BY THE PROUD BAND-MASTER.   *terrupting. To*
                                       be read or sung

And now great gongs whang, *in a heavy*
Sharper, faster, *bass. First*
And kettledrums rattle *eight lines as*
And hide the shame *harsh as pos-*
With a swish and a swirk *sible. Then*
In dead love's name. *gradually*
Red and crimson *musical and*
And scarlet and rose *sonorous.*
Magical poppies
The sweethearts bloom.
The scarlet stays
When the rose-flush goes,
And love lies low
In a marble tomb.
"'Tis the
NIGHT
Of doom,"
Call the ding-dong doom-bells.
" NIGHT
Of Doom,"
Call the ding-dong doom-bells.

Hark how the piccolos still make cheer. *Sharply in-*
    "'Tis a moonlight night in the spring of *terrupting in a*
       the year." *very high key.*

CLANGARANGA, CLANGARANGA, *Heavy bass.*

CLANG . . . CLANG . . . CLANG.

CLANG . . . A . . . RANGA . . .

CLANG . . . A . . . RANGA . . .

CLANG . . . CLANG . . . CLANG . . .

LISTEN . . . TO . . . THE . . . MUSIC . . .

OF . . . THE . . . FIREMEN'S BALL . . .

LISTEN . . . TO . . . THE . . . MUSIC . . .

OF . . . THE . . . FIREMEN'S . . . BALL . . .

SECTION THREE

In Which, contrary to Artistic Custom, the moral of the piece is placed before the reader.

(From the first Khandaka of the Mahavagga: "There Buddha thus addressed his disciples: 'Everything, O mendicants, is burning. With what fire is it burning? I declare unto you it is burning with the fire of passion, with the fire of anger, with the fire of ignorance. It is burning with the anxieties of birth, decay and death, grief, lamentation, suffering and despair. . . . A disciple, . . . becoming weary of all that, divests himself of passion. By absence of passion, he is made free.'")

I once knew a teacher,
Who turned from desire,
Who said to the young men
"Wine is a fire."

To be intoned after the manner of a priestly service.

Who said to the merchants : —
"Gold is a flame
That sears and tortures
If you play at the game."
I once knew a teacher
Who turned from desire
Who said to the soldiers,
"Hate is a fire."
Who said to the statesmen : —
"Power is a flame
That flays and blisters
If you play at the game."
I once knew a teacher
Who turned from desire,
Who said to the lordly,

"Pride is a fire."
Who thus warned the revellers : —
"Life is a flame.
Be cold as the dew
Would you win at the game
With hearts like the stars,
With hearts like the stars."
So BEWARE,
So BEWARE,

*Interrupting
very loudly
for the last
time.*

So BEWARE OF THE FIRE.

Clear the streets,

BOOM, BOOM,

Clear the streets,

BOOM, BOOM,

GIVE THE ENGINES ROOM,

GIVE THE ENGINES ROOM,

LEST SOULS BE TRAPPED

IN A TERRIBLE TOMB.

SAYS THE SWIFT WHITE HORSE

TO THE SWIFT BLACK HORSE: —

"THERE GOES THE ALARM,

THERE GOES THE ALARM.

THEY ARE HITCHED, THEY ARE OFF,

THEY ARE GONE IN A FLASH,

AND THEY STRAIN AT THE DRIVER'S IRON ARM."

CLANG . . . A . . . RANGA, . . . CLANG . . . A

. . . RANGA. . . .

CLANG . . . CLANG . . . CLANG. . . .

CLANG . . . A . . . RANGA. . . . CLANG . . . A

. . . RANGA. . . .

CLANG . . . CLANG . . . CLANG. . . .

CLANG . . . A . . . RANGA. . . . CLANG . . . A

. . . RANGA. . . .

CLANG . . . CLANG . . . *CLANG.* . . .

THE MASTER OF THE DANCE

A chant to which it is intended a group of children shall dance and improvise pantomime led by their dancing-teacher.

I

A master deep-eyed
Ere his manhood was ripe,
He sang like a thrush,
He could play any pipe.
So dull in the school
That he scarcely could spell,
He read but a bit,
And he figured not well.
A bare-footed fool,
Shod only with grace;
Long hair streaming down
Round a wind-hardened face;
He smiled like a girl,
Or like clear winter skies,
A virginal light
Making stars of his eyes.

In swiftness and poise,
A proud child of the deer,
A white fawn he was,
Yet a fawn without fear.
No youth thought him vain,
Or made mock of his hair,
Or laughed when his ways
Were most curiously fair.
A mastiff at fight,
He could strike to the earth
The envious one
Who would challenge his worth.
However we bowed
To the schoolmaster mild,
Our spirits went out
To the fawn-footed child.
His beckoning led
Our troop to the brush.
We found nothing there
But a wind and a hush.
He sat by a stone
And he looked on the ground,
As if in the weeds
There was something profound.
His pipe seemed to neigh,

Then to bleat like a sheep,
Then sound like a stream
Or a waterfall deep.
It whispered strange tales,
Human words it spoke not.
Told fair things to come,
And our marvellous lot
If now with fawn-steps
Unshod we advanced
To the midst of the grove
And in reverence danced.
We obeyed as he piped
Soft grass to young feet,
Was a medicine mighty,
A remedy meet.
Our thin blood awoke,
It grew dizzy and wild,
Though scarcely a word
Moved the lips of a child.
Our dance gave allegiance,
It set us apart,
We tripped a strange measure,
Uplifted of heart.

D

II

We thought to be proud
Of our fawn everywhere.
We could hardly see how
Simple books were a care.
No rule of the school
This strange student could tame.
He was banished one day,
While we quivered with shame.
He piped back our love
On a moon-silvered night,
Enticed us once more
To the place of delight.
A greeting he sang
And it made our blood beat,
It tramped upon custom
And mocked at defeat.
He builded a fire
And we tripped in a ring,
The embers our books
And the fawn our good king.
And now we approached
All the mysteries rare
That shadowed his eyelids

And blew through his hair.
That spell now was peace
The deep strength of the trees,
The children of nature
We clambered her knees.
Our breath and our moods
Were in tune with her own,
Tremendous her presence,
Eternal her throne.
The ostracized child
Our white foreheads kissed,
Our bodies and souls
Became lighter than mist.
Sweet dresses like snow
Our small lady-loves wore,
Like moonlight the thoughts
That our bosoms upbore.
Like a lily the touch
Of each cold little hand.
The loves of the stars
We could now understand.
O quivering air !
O the crystalline night !
O pauses of awe
And the faces swan-white !

O ferns in the dusk !
O forest-shrined hour !
O earth that sent upward
The thrill and the power,
To lift us like leaves,
A delirious whirl,
The masterful boy
And the delicate girl !
What child that strange night-time
Can ever forget ?
His fealty due
And his infinite debt
To the folly divine,
To the exquisite rule
Of the perilous master,
The fawn-footed fool ?

III

Now soldiers we seem,
And night brings a new thing,
A terrible ire,
As of thunder awing.
A warrior power,
That old chivalry stirred,
When knights took up arms,

As the maidens gave word.
THE END OF OUR WAR,
WILL BE GLORY UNTOLD.
WHEN THE TOWN LIKE A GREAT
BUDDING ROSE SHALL UNFOLD!
Near, nearer that war,
And that ecstasy comes,
We hear the trees beating
Invisible drums.
The fields of the night
Are starlit above,
Our girls are white torches
Of conquest and love.
No nerve without will,
And no breast without breath,
We whirl with the planets
That never know death!

THE MYSTERIOUS CAT

A chant for a children's pantomime dance, suggested by a picture painted by George Mather Richards.

I saw a proud, mysterious cat,
I saw a proud, mysterious cat
Too proud to catch a mouse or rat —
Mew, mew, mew.

But catnip she would eat, and purr,
But catnip she would eat, and purr.
And goldfish she did much prefer —
Mew, mew, mew.

I saw a cat — 'twas but a dream,
I saw a cat — 'twas but a dream
Who scorned the slave that brought her
    cream —
Mew, mew, mew.

Unless the slave were dressed in style,
Unless the slave were dressed in style

And knelt before her all the while —
Mew, mew, mew.

Did you ever hear of a thing like that?
Did you ever hear of a thing like that?
Did you ever hear of a thing like that?
Oh, what a proud mysterious cat.
Oh, what a proud mysterious cat.
Oh, what a proud mysterious cat.
Mew . . . mew . . . mew.

A DIRGE FOR A RIGHTEOUS KITTEN

To be intoned, all but the two italicized lines, which are to be spoken in a snappy, matter-of-fact way.

Ding-dong, ding-dong, ding-dong.
Here lies a kitten good, who kept
A kitten's proper place.
He stole no pantry eatables,
Nor scratched the baby's face.
He let the alley-cats alone.
He had no yowling vice.
His shirt was always laundried well,
He freed the house of mice.
Until his death he had not caused
His little mistress tears,
He wore his ribbon prettily,
He washed behind his ears.
Ding-dong, ding-dong, ding-dong.

YANKEE DOODLE

This poem is intended as a description of a sort of Blashfield mural painting on the sky. To be sung to the tune of Yankee Doodle, yet in a slower, more orotund fashion. It is presumably an exercise for an entertainment on the evening of Washington's Birthday.

Dawn this morning burned all red
Watching them in wonder.
There I saw our spangled flag
Divide the clouds asunder.
Then there followed Washington.
Ah, he rode from glory,
Cold and mighty as his name
And stern as Freedom's story.
Unsubdued by burning dawn
Led his continentals.
Vast they were, and strange to see
In gray old regimentals : —
Marching still with bleeding feet,
Bleeding feet and jesting —

Marching from the judgment throne
With energy unresting.
How their merry quickstep played —
Silver, sharp, sonorous,
Piercing through with prophecy
The demons' rumbling chorus —
Behold the ancient powers of sin
And slavery before them ! —
Sworn to stop the glorious dawn,
The pit-black clouds hung o'er them.
Plagues that rose to blast the day
Fiend and tiger faces,
Monsters plotting bloodshed for
The patient toiling races.
Round the dawn their cannon raged,
Hurling bolts of thunder,
Yet before our spangled flag
Their host was cut asunder.
Like a mist they fled away. . . .
Ended wrath and roaring.
Still our restless soldier-host
From East to West went pouring.

High beside the sun of noon
They bore our banner splendid.

All its days of stain and shame
And heaviness were ended.
Men were swelling now the throng
From great and lowly station —
Valiant citizens to-day
Of every tribe and nation.
Not till night their rear-guard came,
Down the west went marching,
And left behind the sunset-rays
In beauty overarching.
War-god banners lead us still,
Rob, enslave and harry
Let us rather choose to-day
The flag the angels carry —
Flag we love, but brighter far —
Soul of it made splendid :
Let its days of stain and shame
And heaviness be ended.
Let its fifes fill all the sky,
Redeemed souls marching after,
Hills and mountains shake with song,
While seas roll on in laughter.

THE BLACK HAWK WAR OF THE ARTISTS

WRITTEN FOR LORADO TAFT'S STATUE OF BLACK HAWK
AT OREGON, ILLINOIS

To be given in the manner of the Indian Oration and
the Indian War-Cry.

Hawk of the Rocks,
Yours is our cause to-day.
Watching your foes
Here in our war array,
Young men we stand,
Wolves of the West at bay.

> *Power, power for war*
> *Comes from these trees divine;*
> *Power from the boughs,*
> *Boughs where the dew-beads shine,*
> *Power from the cones —*
> *Yea, from the breath of the pine !*

Power to restore
All that the white hand mars.

See the dead east
Crushed with the iron cars —
Chimneys black
Blinding the sun and stars !

Hawk of the pines,
Hawk of the plain-winds fleet,
You shall be king
There in the iron street,
Factory and forge
Trodden beneath your feet.

There will proud trees
Grow as they grow by streams.
There will proud thoughts
Walk as in warrior dreams.
There will proud deeds
Bloom as when battle gleams !

Warriors of Art,
We will hold council there,
Hewing in stone
Things to the trapper fair,
Painting the gray
Veils that the spring moons wear,

This our revenge,
This one tremendous change :
Making new towns,
Lit with a star-fire strange,
Wild as the dawn
Gilding the bison-range.

All the young men
Chanting your cause that day,
Red-men, new-made
Out of the Saxon clay,
Strong and redeemed,
Bold in your war-array !

THE JINGO AND THE MINSTREL

AN ARGUMENT FOR THE MAINTENANCE OF PEACE AND
GOODWILL WITH THE JAPANESE PEOPLE

Glossary for the uninstructed and the hasty: Jimmu
Tenno, ancestor of all the Japanese Emperors; Nikko,
Japan's loveliest shrine; Iyeyasu, her greatest statesman;
Bushido, her code of knighthood; The Forty-seven
Ronins, her classic heroes; Nogi, her latest hero; Fuji,
her most beautiful mountain.

"Now do you know of Avalon *The minstrel*
 That sailors call Japan?   *speaks.*
She holds as rare a chivalry
 As ever bled for man.
King Arthur sleeps at Nikko hill
 Where Iyeyasu lies,
And there the broad Pendragon flag
 In deathless splendor flies."

"Nay, minstrel, but the great ships come *The jingo*
 From out the sunset sea.   *answers.*
We cannot greet the souls they bring

With welcome high and free.
How can the Nippon nondescripts
That weird and dreadful band
Be aught but what we find them here: —
The blasters of the land?"

"First race, first men from anywhere
   To face you, eye to eye.
For *that* do you curse Avalon
   And raise a hue and cry?
These toilers cannot kiss your hand,
   Or fawn with hearts bowed down.
Be glad for them, and Avalon,
   And Arthur's ghostly crown.

The minstrel replies.

"No doubt your guests, with sage debate
   In grave things gentlemen
Will let your trade and farms alone
   And turn them back again.
But why should brawling braggarts rise
   With hasty words of shame
To drive them back like dogs and swine
   Who in due honor came?"

"We cannot give them honor, sir.
   We give them scorn for scorn.

The jingo answers.

And Rumor steals around the world
  All white-skinned men to warn
Against this sleek silk-merchant here
  And viler coolie-man
And wrath within the courts of war
  Brews on against Japan!"

"Must Avalon, with hope forlorn,   *The minstrel*
  Her back against the wall,   *replies.*
Have lived her brilliant life in vain
  While ruder tribes take all?
Must Arthur stand with Asian Celts,
  A ghost with spear and crown,
Behind the great Pendragon flag
  And be again cut down?

"Tho Europe's self shall move against
  High Jimmu Tenno's throne
The Forty-seven Ronin Men
  Will not be found alone.
For Percival and Bedivere
  And Nogi side by side
Will stand, — with mourning Merlin there,
  Tho all go down in pride.

E

"But has the world the envious dream —
  Ah, such things cannot be, —
To tear their fairy-land like silk
  And toss it in the sea ?
Must venom rob the future day
  The ultimate world-man
Of rare Bushido, code of codes,
  The fair heart of Japan ?

"Go, be the guest of Avalon.
  Believe me, it lies there
Behind the mighty gray sea-wall
  Where heathen bend in prayer :
Where peasants lift adoring eyes
  To Fuji's crown of snow.
King Arthur's knights will be your hosts,
  So cleanse your heart, and go.

"And you will find but gardens sweet
  Prepared beyond the seas,
And you will find but gentlefolk
  Beneath the cherry-trees.
So walk you worthy of your Christ
  Tho church bells do not sound,
And weave the bands of brotherhood
  On Jimmu Tenno's ground."

I HEARD IMMANUEL SINGING

(The poem shows the Master, with his work done, singing to free his heart in Heaven.)

This poem is intended to be half said, half sung, very softly, to the well-known tune: —

"Last night I lay a-sleeping,
There came a dream so fair,
I stood in Old Jerusalem
Beside the temple there, —" etc.

Yet this tune is not to be fitted on, arbitrarily. It is here given to suggest the manner of handling rather than determine it.

I heard Immanuel singing   *To be sung.*
Within his own good lands,
I saw him bend above his harp.
I watched his wandering hands
Lost amid the harp-strings;
Sweet, sweet I heard him play.
His wounds were altogether healed.
Old things had passed away.

All things were new, but music.
The blood of David ran
Within the Son of David,
Our God, the Son of Man.
He was ruddy like a shepherd.
His bold young face, how fair.
Apollo of the silver bow
Had not such flowing hair.

I saw Immanuel singing
On a tree-girdled hill.
The glad remembering branches
Dimly echoed still
The grand new song proclaiming
The Lamb that had been slain.
New-built, the Holy City
Gleamed in the murmuring plain.

To be read very softly, but in spirited response.

The crowning hours were over.
The pageants all were past.
Within the many mansions
The hosts, grown still at last,
In homes of holy mystery
Slept long by crooning springs

Or waked to peaceful glory,
A universe of Kings.

He left his people happy.   *To be sung.*
He wandered free to sigh
Alone in lowly friendship
With the green grass and the sky.
He murmured ancient music
His red heart burned to sing
Because his perfect conquest
Had grown a weary thing.

No chant of gilded triumph —
His lonely song was made
Of Art's deliberate freedom;
Of minor chords arrayed
In soft and shadowy colors
That once were radiant flowers : —
The Rose of Sharon, bleeding
In Olive-shadowed bowers : —

And all the other roses
In the songs of East and West
Of love and war and worshipping,
And every shield and crest

Of thistle or of lotus
Or sacred lily wrought
In creeds and psalms and palaces
And temples of white thought : —

All these he sang, half-smiling   *To be read very*
                                          softly, yet in
And weeping as he smiled,   *spirited re-*
                                          sponse.
Laughing, talking to his harp
As to a new-born child : —
As though the arts forgotten
But bloomed to prophecy
These careless, fearless harp-strings,
New-crying in the sky.
"When this his hour of sorrow   *To be sung.*
For flowers and Arts of men
Has passed in ghostly music,"
I asked my wild heart then —
What will he sing to-morrow,
What wonder, all his own
Alone, set free, rejoicing,
With a green hill for his throne ?
What will he sing to-morrow
What wonder all his own
Alone, set free, rejoicing,
With a green hill for his throne ?

SECOND SECTION

INCENSE

AN ARGUMENT

I. The Voice of the Man Impatient with Visions and Utopias

We find your soft Utopias as white
As new-cut bread, and dull as life in cells,
O, scribes who dare forget how wild we are
How human breasts adore alarum bells.
You house us in a hive of prigs and saints
Communal, frugal, clean and chaste by law.
I'd rather brood in bloody Elsinore
Or be Lear's fool, straw-crowned amid the
    straw.
Promise us all our share in Agincourt
Say that our clerks shall venture scorns and
    death,
That future ant-hills will not be too good
For Henry Fifth, or Hotspur, or Macbeth.
Promise that through to-morrow's spirit-war
Man's deathless soul will hack and hew its
    way,
Each flaunting Cæsar climbing to his fate
Scorning the utmost steps of yesterday.

57

Never a shallow jester any more !
Let not Jack Falstaff spill the ale in vain.
Let Touchstone set the fashions for the wise
And Ariel wreak his fancies through the rain.

II. The Rhymer's Reply.   Incense and Splendor

Incense and Splendor haunt me as I go.
Though my good works have been, alas, too
      few,
Though I do naught, High Heaven comes
      down to me,
And future ages pass in tall review.
I see the years to come as armies vast,
Stalking tremendous through the fields of
      time.
Man is unborn.   To-morrow he is born,
Flame-like to hover o'er the moil and grime,
Striving, aspiring till the shame is gone,
Sowing a million flowers, where now we
      mourn —
Laying new, precious pavements with a song,
Founding new shrines, the good streets to
      adorn.
I have seen lovers by those new-built walls

Clothed like the dawn in orange, gold and
  red.
Eyes flashing forth the glory-light of love
Under the wreaths that crowned each royal
  head.
Life was made greater by their sweetheart
  prayers.
Passion was turned to civic strength that
  day —
Piling the marbles, making fairer domes
With zeal that else had burned bright youth
  away.
I have seen priestesses of life go by
Gliding in samite through the incense-sea —
Innocent children marching with them there,
Singing in flowered robes, "THE EARTH IS
  FREE":
While on the fair, deep-carved unfinished
  towers
Sentinels watched in armor, night and day —
Guarding the brazier-fires of hope and
  dream —
Wild was their peace, and dawn-bright their
  array !

A RHYME ABOUT AN ELECTRICAL
ADVERTISING SIGN

I look on the specious electrical light
Blatant, mechanical, crawling and white,
Wickedly red or malignantly green
Like the beads of a young Senegambian
    queen.
Showing, while millions of souls hurry on,
The virtues of collars, from sunset till
    dawn,
By dart or by tumble of whirl within whirl,
Starting new fads for the shame-weary girl,
By maggoty motions in sickening line
Proclaiming a hat or a soup or a wine,
While there far above the steep cliffs of the
    street
The stars sing a message elusive and sweet.

Now man cannot rest in his pleasure and
    toil
His clumsy contraptions of coil upon coil

Till the thing he invents, in its use and its
    range,
Leads on to the marvellous CHANGE BEYOND
    CHANGE.
Some day this old Broadway shall climb to
    the skies,
As a ribbon of cloud on a soul-wind shall rise.
And we shall be lifted, rejoicing by night,
Till we join with the planets who choir their
    delight.
The signs in the street and the signs in the
    skies
Shall make a new Zodiac, guiding the wise,
And Broadway make one with that marvel-
    lous stair
That is climbed by the rainbow-clad spirits
    of prayer.

IN MEMORY OF A CHILD

The angels guide him now,
And watch his curly head,
And lead him in their games,
The little boy we led.

He cannot come to harm,
He knows more than we know,
His light is brighter far
Than daytime here below.

His path leads on and on,
Through pleasant lawns and flowers,
His brown eyes open wide
At grass more green than ours.

With playmates like himself,
The shining boy will sing,
Exploring wondrous woods,
Sweet with eternal spring.

GALAHAD, KNIGHT WHO PERISHED

A Poem Dedicated to All Crusaders against the International and Interstate Traffic in Young Girls

Galahad . . . soldier that perished . . . ages
    ago,
Our hearts are breaking with shame, our
    tears overflow.
Galahad . . . knight who perished . . .
    awaken again,
Teach us to fight for immaculate ways
    among men.
Soldiers fantastic, we pray to the star of the
    sea,
We pray to the mother of God that the
    bound may be free.
Rose-crowned lady from heaven, give us thy
    grace,
Help us the intricate, desperate battle to
    face

Till the leer of the trader is seen nevermore
in the land,
Till we bring every maid of the age to one
sheltering hand.
Ah, they are priceless, the pale and the ivory
and red !
Breathless we gaze on the curls of each
glorious head !
Arm them with strength mediæval, thy marvellous dower,
Blast now their tempters, shelter their steps
with thy power.
Leave not life's fairest to perish — strangers
to thee,
Let not the weakest be shipwrecked, oh,
star of the sea !

THE LEADEN-EYED

Let not young souls be smothered out before
They do quaint deeds and fully flaunt their
    pride.
It is the world's one crime its babes grow
    dull,
Its poor are ox-like, limp and leaden-eyed.
Not that they starve, but starve so dream-
    lessly,
Not that they sow, but that they seldom
    reap,
Not that they serve, but have no gods to
    serve,
Not that they die, but that they die like
    sheep.

F

AN INDIAN SUMMER DAY ON THE PRAIRIE

(IN THE BEGINNING)

The sun is a huntress young,
The sun is a red, red joy,
The sun is an Indian girl,
Of the tribe of the Illinois.

(MID-MORNING)

The sun is a smouldering fire,
That creeps through the high gray plain,
And leaves not a bush of cloud
To blossom with flowers of rain.

(NOON)

The sun is a wounded deer,
That treads pale grass in the skies,
Shaking his golden horns,
Flashing his baleful eyes.

(SUNSET)

The sun is an eagle old,
There in the windless west.
Atop of the spirit-cliffs
He builds him a crimson nest.

THE HEARTH ETERNAL

There dwelt a widow learned and devout,
Behind our hamlet on the eastern hill.
Three sons she had, who went to find the
  world.
They promised to return, but wandered
  still.
The cities used them well, they won their
  way,
Rich gifts they sent, to still their mother's
  sighs.
Worn out with honors, and apart from her,
They died as many a self-made exile dies.
The mother had a hearth that would not
  quench,
The deathless embers fought the creeping
  gloom.
She said to us who came with wondering
  eyes —
"This is a magic fire, a magic room."
The pine burned out, but still the coals
  glowed on,

Her grave grew old beneath the pear-tree
    shade,
And yet her crumbling home enshrined the
    light.
The neighbors peering in were half afraid.
Then sturdy beggars, needing fagots, came,
One at a time, and stole the walls, and floor.
They left a naked stone, but how it blazed!
And in the thunderstorm it flared the more.
And now it was that men were heard to
    say,
"This light should be beloved by all the
    town."
At last they made the slope a place of prayer,
Where marvellous thoughts from God came
    sweeping down.
They left their churches crumbling in the
    sun,
They met on that soft hill, one brotherhood;
One strength and valor only, one delight,
One laughing, brooding genius, great and
    good.
Now many gray-haired prodigals come
    home,
The place out-flames the cities of the land,

And twice-born Brahmans reach us from
    afar,
With subtle eyes prepared to understand.
Higher and higher burns the eastern steep,
Showing the roads that march from every
    place,
A steady beacon o'er the weary leagues,
At dead of night it lights the traveller's face !
Thus has the widow conquered half the
    earth,
She who increased in faith, though all alone,
Who kept her empty house a magic place,
Has made the town a holy angel's throne.

THE SOUL OF THE CITY RECEIVES THE GIFT OF THE HOLY SPIRIT

A BROADSIDE DISTRIBUTED IN SPRINGFIELD, ILLINOIS

Censers are swinging
Over the town;
Censers are swinging,
Look overhead !
Censers are swinging,
Heaven comes down.
City, dead city,
Awake from the dead !

Censers, tremendous,
Gleam overhead.
Wind-harps are ringing,
Wind-harps unseen —
Calling and calling : —
"Wake from the dead.
Rise, little city,
Shine like a queen."

Soldiers of Christ
For battle grow keen.
Heaven-sent winds
Haunt alley and lane.
Singing of life
In town-meadows green
After the toil
And battle and pain.

Incense is pouring
Like the spring rain
Down on the mob
That moil through the street.
Blessed are they
Who behold it and gain
Power made more mighty
Thro' every defeat.

Builders, toil on.
Make all complete.
Make Springfield wonderful.
Make her renown
Worthy this day,
Till, at God's feet,
Tranced, saved forever,
Waits the white town.

Censers are swinging
Over the town,
Censers gigantic !
Look overhead !
Hear the winds singing : —
"Heaven comes down.
City, dead city,
Awake from the dead."

BY THE SPRING, AT SUNSET

Sometimes we remember kisses,
Remember the dear heart-leap when they
     came:
Not always, but sometimes we remember
The kindness, the dumbness, the good flame
Of laughter and farewell.

                           Beside the road
Afar from those who said "Good-by" I
     write,
Far from my city task, my lawful load.

Sun in my face, wind beside my shoulder,
Streaming clouds, banners of new-born night
Enchant me now. The splendors growing
     bolder
Make bold my soul for some new wise de-
     light.

I write the day's event, and quench my
     drouth,
Pausing beside the spring with happy mind.
And now I feel those kisses on my mouth,
Hers most of all, one little friend most kind.

I WENT DOWN INTO THE DESERT

I went down into the desert
To meet Elijah —
Arisen from the dead.
I thought to find him in an echoing cave;
For so my dream had said.

I went down into the desert
To meet John the Baptist.
I walked with feet that bled,
Seeking that prophet lean and brown and
    bold.
I spied foul fiends instead.

I went down into the desert
To meet my God.
By him be comforted.
I went down into the desert
To meet my God.
And I met the devil in red.

I went down into the desert
To meet my God.

O, Lord my God, awaken from the dead !
I see you there, your thorn-crown on the
    ground,
I see you there, half-buried in the sand.
I see you there, your white bones glistening,
    bare,
The carrion-birds a-wheeling round your head.

LOVE AND LAW

True Love is founded in rocks of Remem-
    brance
In stones of Forbearance and mortar of
    Pain.
The workman lays wearily granite on
    granite,
And bleeds for his castle 'mid sunshine and
    rain.

Love is not velvet, not all of it velvet,
Not all of it banners, not gold-leaf alone.
'Tis stern as the ages and old as Religion.
With Patience its watchword, and Law for
    its throne.

THE PERFECT MARRIAGE

I

I hate this yoke; for the world's sake here
    put it on:
Knowing 'twill weigh as much on you till
    life is gone.
Knowing you love your freedom dear, as I
    love mine —
Knowing that love unchained has been our
    life's great wine:
Our one great wine (yet spent too soon, and
    serving none;
Of the two cups free love at last the deadly
    one).

II

We grant our meetings will be tame, not
    honey-sweet
No longer turning to the tryst with flying
    feet.
We know the toil that now must come will
    spoil the bloom

And tenderness of passion's touch, and in its
    room
Will come tame habit, deadly calm, sorrow
    and gloom.
Oh, how the battle scars the best who enter
    life !
Each soldier comes out blind or lame from
    the black strife.
Mad or diseased or damned of soul the best
    may come —
It matters not how merrily now rolls the
    drum,
The fife shrills high, the horn sings loud, till
    no steps lag —
And all adore that silken flame, Desire's
    great flag.

III

We will build strong our tiny fort, strong as
    we can —
Holding one inner room beyond the sword
    of man.
Love is too wide, it seems to-day, to hide it
    there.
It seems to flood the fields of corn, and gild
    the air —

It seems to breathe from every brook, from
    flowers to sigh —

It seems a cataract poured down from the
    great sky;

It seems a tenderness so vast no bush but
    shows

Its haunting and transfiguring light where
    wonder glows.

It wraps us in a silken snare by shadowy
    streams,

And wildering sweet and stung with joy
    your white soul seems

A flame, a flame, conquering day, conquer-
    ing night,

Brought from our God, a holy thing, a mad
    delight.

But love, when all things beat it down,
    leaves the wide air,

The heavens are gray, and men turn wolves,
    lean with despair.

Ah, when we need love most, and weep,
    when all is dark,

Love is a pinch of ashes gray, with one live
    spark —

Yet on the hope to keep alive that treasure
 strange
Hangs all earth's struggle, strife and scorn,
 and desperate change.

IV

Love? . . . we will scarcely love our babes
 full many a time —
Knowing their souls and ours too well, and
 all our grime —
And there beside our holy hearth we'll hide
 our eyes —
Lest we should flash what seems disdain
 without disguise.
Yet there shall be no wavering there in that
 deep trial —
And no false fire or stranger hand or traitor
 vile —
We'll fight the gloom and fight the world
 with strong sword-play,
Entrenched within our block-house small,
 ever at bay —
As fellow-warriors, underpaid, wounded and
 wild,
True to their battered flag, their faith still
 undefiled!

DARLING DAUGHTER OF BABYLON

Too soon you wearied of our tears.
And then you danced with spangled feet,
Leading Belshazzar's chattering court
A-tinkling through the shadowy street.
With mead they came, with chants of shame.
DESIRE'S red flag before them flew.
And Istar's music moved your mouth
And Baal's deep shames rewoke in you.

Now you could drive the royal car;
Forget our Nation's breaking load:
Now you could sleep on silver beds —
(Bitter and dark was our abode.)
And so, for many a night you laughed,
And knew not of my hopeless prayer,
Till God's own spirit whipped you forth
From Istar's shrine, from Istar's stair.

Darling daughter of Babylon —
Rose by the black Euphrates flood —

G

Again your beauty grew more dear
Than my slave's bread, than my heart's
blood.
We sang of Zion, good to know,
Where righteousness and peace abide. . . .
What of your second sacrilege
Carousing at Belshazzar's side?

Once, by a stream, we clasped tired hands—
Your paint and henna washed away.
Your place, you said, was with the slaves
Who sewed the thick cloth, night and day.
You were a pale and holy maid
Toil-bound with us.   One night you said: —
"Your God shall be my God until
I slumber with the patriarch dead."

Pardon, daughter of Babylon,
If, on this night remembering
Our lover walks under the walls
Of hanging gardens in the spring,
A venom comes from broken hope,
From memories of your comrade-song
Until I curse your painted eyes
And do your flower-mouth too much wrong.

THE AMARANTH

Ah, in the night, all music haunts me
    here. . . .
Is it for naught high Heaven cracks and
    yawns
And the tremendous Amaranth descends
Sweet with the glory of ten thousand dawns?

Does it not mean my God would have me
    say : —
"Whether you will or no, O city young,
Heaven will bloom like one great flower for
    you,
Flash and loom greatly all your marts
    among?"

Friends, I will not cease hoping though you
    weep.
Such things I see, and some of them shall
    come

Though now our streets are harsh and ashen-
    gray,
Though our strong youths are strident now,
    or dumb.
Friends, that sweet town, that wonder-town,
    shall rise.
Naught can delay it.   Though it may not
    be
Just as I dream, it comes at last I know
With streets like channels of an incense-sea.

THE ALCHEMIST'S PETITION

Thou wilt not sentence to eternal life
My soul that prays that it may sleep and
    sleep
Like a white statue dropped into the deep,
Covered with sand, covered with chests of
    gold,
And slave-bones, tossed from many a pirate
    hold.

But for this prayer thou wilt not bind in
    Hell
My soul, that shook with love for Fame and
    Truth —
In such unquenched desires consumed his
    youth —
Let me turn dust, like dead leaves in the
    Fall,
Or wood that lights an hour your knightly
    hall —
                    Amen.

TWO EASTER STANZAS

I

The Hope of the Resurrection

Though I have watched so many mourners
    weep
O'er the real dead, in dull earth laid asleep —
Those dead seemed but the shadows of my
    days
That passed and left me in the sun's bright
    rays.
Now though you go on smiling in the sun
Our love is slain, and love and you were one.
You are the first, you I have known so long,
Whose death was deadly, a tremendous
    wrong.
Therefore I seek the faith that sets it right
Amid the lilies and the candle-light.
I think on Heaven, for in that air so clear
We two may meet, confused and parted
    here.

Ah, when man's dearest dies, 'tis then he
    goes
To that old balm that heals the centuries'
    woes.
Then Christ's wild cry in all the streets is
    rife : —
"I am the Resurrection and the Life."

II

WE MEET AT THE JUDGMENT AND I FEAR IT NOT

Though better men may fear that trumpet's
    warning,
I meet you, lady, on the Judgment morning,
With golden hope my spirit still adorning.

Our God who made you all so fair and sweet
Is three times gentle, and before his feet
Rejoicing I shall say : — "The girl you gave
Was my first Heaven, an angel bent to save.
Oh, God, her maker, if my ingrate breath
Is worth this rescue from the Second Death,
Perhaps her dear proud eyes grow gentler too
That scorned my graceless years and trophies
    few.

Gone are those years, and gone ill-deeds that
 turned
Her sacred beauty from my songs that
 burned.
We now as comrades through the stars
 may take
The rich and arduous quests I did forsake.
Grant me a seraph-guide to thread the
 throng
And quickly find that woman-soul so strong.
I dream that in her deeply-hidden heart
Hurt love lived on, though we were far
 apart,
A brooding secret mercy like your own
That blooms to-day to vindicate your
 throne.

THE TRAVELLER-HEART

(To a Man who maintained that the Mausoleum is the
Stateliest Possible Manner of Interment)

I would be one with the dark, dark earth : —
Follow the plough with a yokel tread.
I would be part of the Indian corn,
Walking the rows with the plumes o'erhead.

I would be one with the lavish earth,
Eating the bee-stung apples red :
Walking where lambs walk on the hills ;
By oak-grove paths to the pools be led.

I would be one with the dark-bright night
When sparkling skies and the lightning
    wed —
Walking on with the vicious wind
By roads whence even the dogs have fled.

I would be one with the sacred earth
On to the end, till I sleep with the dead.

Terror shall put no spears through me.
Peace shall jewel my shroud instead.

I shall be one with all pit-black things
Finding their lowering threat unsaid:
Stars for my pillow there in the gloom, —
Oak-roots arching about my head!

Stars, like daisies, shall rise through the
      earth,
Acorns fall round my breast that bled.
Children shall weave there a flowery chain,
Squirrels on acorn-hearts be fed: —

Fruit of the traveller-heart of me,
Fruit of my harvest-songs long sped:
Sweet with the life of my sunburned days
When the sheaves were ripe, and the apples
      red.

THE NORTH STAR WHISPERS TO THE
BLACKSMITH'S SON

The North Star whispers: "You are one
Of those whose course no chance can change.
You blunder, but are not undone,
Your spirit-task is fixed and strange.

"When here you walk, a bloodless shade,
A singer all men else forget.
Your chants of hammer, forge and spade
Will move the prairie-village yet.

"That young, stiff-necked, reviling town
Beholds your fancies on her walls,
And paints them out or tears them down,
Or bars them from her feasting-halls.

"Yet shall the fragments still remain;
Yet shall remain some watch-tower strong
That ivy-vines will not disdain,
Haunted and trembling with your song.

"Your flambeau in the dusk shall burn,
Flame high in storms, flame white and
    clear;
Your ghost in gleaming robes return
And burn a deathless incense here."

THIRD SECTION

A MISCELLANY CALLED "THE CHRISTMAS TREE"

THIS SECTION IS A CHRISTMAS TREE

This section is a Christmas tree:
Loaded with pretty toys for you.
Behold the blocks, the Noah's arks,
The popguns painted red and blue.
No solemn pine-cone forest-fruit,
But silver horns and candy sacks
And many little tinsel hearts
And cherubs pink, and jumping-jacks.
For every child a gift, I hope.
The doll upon the topmost bough
Is mine.   But all the rest are yours.
And I will light the candles now.

THE SUN SAYS HIS PRAYERS

"The sun says his prayers," said the fairy,
Or else he would wither and die.
"The sun says his prayers," said the fairy,
"For strength to climb up through the sky.
He leans on invisible angels,
And Faith is his prop and his rod.
The sky is his crystal cathedral.
And dawn is his altar to God."

POPCORN, GLASS BALLS, AND CRANBERRIES
(AS IT WERE)

I. THE LION

The Lion is a kingly beast.
He likes a Hindu for a feast.
And if no Hindu he can get,
The lion-family is upset.

He cuffs his wife and bites her ears
Till she is nearly moved to tears.
Then some explorer finds the den
And all is family peace again.

II. AN EXPLANATION OF THE GRASSHOPPER

The Grasshopper, the grasshopper,
I will explain to you: —
He is the Brownies' racehorse,
The fairies' Kangaroo.

III. THE DANGEROUS LITTLE BOY FAIRIES

In fairyland the little boys
Would rather fight than eat their meals.

H

They like to chase a gauze-winged fly
And catch and beat him till he squeals.
Sometimes they come to sleeping men
Armed with the deadly red-rose thorn,
And those that feel its fearful wound
Repent the day that they were born.

IV. THE MOUSE THAT GNAWED THE OAK-TREE DOWN

The mouse that gnawed the oak-tree down
Began his task in early life.
He kept so busy with his teeth
He had no time to take a wife.

He gnawed and gnawed through sun and
    rain
When the ambitious fit was on,
Then rested in the sawdust till
A month of idleness had gone.

He did not move about to hunt
The coteries of mousie-men.
He was a snail-paced, stupid thing
Until he cared to gnaw again.

The mouse that gnawed the oak-tree down,
When that tough foe was at his feet —

Found in the stump no angel-cake
Nor buttered bread, nor cheese, nor meat —
The forest-roof let in the sky.
"This light is worth the work," said he.
"I'll make this ancient swamp more light,"
And started on another tree.

V. PARVENU

Where does Cinderella sleep?
By far-off day-dream river.
A secret place her burning Prince
Decks, while his heart-strings quiver.

Homesick for our cinder world,
Her low-born shoulders shiver;
She longs for sleep in cinders curled —
We, for the day-dream river.

VI. THE SPIDER AND THE GHOST OF THE FLY

Once I loved a spider
When I was born a fly,
A velvet-footed spider
With a gown of rainbow-dye.
She ate my wings and gloated.
She bound me with a hair.

She drove me to her parlor
Above her winding stair.
To educate young spiders
She took me all apart.
My ghost came back to haunt her.
I saw her eat my heart.

VII. CRICKETS ON A STRIKE

The foolish queen of fairyland
From her milk-white throne in a lily-bell,
Gave command to her cricket-band
To play for her when the dew-drops fell.

But the cold dew spoiled their instruments
And they play for the foolish queen no more.
Instead those sturdy malcontents
Play sharps and flats in my kitchen floor.

HOW A LITTLE GIRL DANCED

DEDICATED TO LUCY BATES

(Being a reminiscence of certain private theatricals.)

Oh, cabaret dancer, *I* know a dancer,
Whose eyes have not looked on the feasts
that are vain.
I know a dancer, *I* know a dancer,
Whose soul has no bond with the beasts of
the plain :
Judith the dancer, Judith the dancer,
With foot like the snow, and with step like
the rain.

Oh, thrice-painted dancer, vaudeville dancer,
Sad in your spangles, with soul all astrain,
I know a dancer, *I* know a dancer,
Whose laughter and weeping are spiritual
gain,
A pure-hearted, high-hearted maiden
evangel,

With strength the dark cynical earth to dis-
    dain.

Flowers of bright Broadway, you of the
    chorus,
Who sing in the hope of forgetting your pain:
I turn to a sister of Sainted Cecilia,
A white bird escaping the earth's tangled
    skein: —
The music of God is her innermost brooding,
The whispering angels her footsteps sustain.

Oh, proud Russian dancer: praise for your
    dancing.
No clean human passion my rhyme would
    arraign.
You dance for Apollo with noble devotion,
A high cleansing revel to make the heart sane.
But Judith the dancer prays to a spirit
More white than Apollo and all of his train.

I know a dancer who finds the true Godhead,
Who bends o'er a brazier in Heaven's clear
    plain.
I know a dancer, I know a dancer,

Who lifts us toward peace, from this earth
    that is vain:
Judith the dancer, Judith the dancer,
With foot like the snow, and with step like
    the rain.

IN PRAISE OF SONGS THAT DIE

AFTER HAVING READ A GREAT DEAL OF GOOD CURRENT POETRY IN THE MAGAZINES AND NEWSPAPERS

Ah, they are passing, passing by,
Wonderful songs, but born to die!
Cries from the infinite human seas,
Waves thrice-winged with harmonies.
Here I stand on a pier in the foam
Seeing the songs to the beach go home,
Dying in sand while the tide flows back,
As it flowed of old in its fated track.
Oh, hurrying tide that will not hear
Your own foam-children dying near:
Is there no refuge-house of song,
No home, no haven where songs belong?
Oh, precious hymns that come and go!
You perish, and I love you so!

FACTORY WINDOWS ARE ALWAYS BROKEN

Factory windows are always broken.
Somebody's always throwing bricks,
Somebody's always heaving cinders,
Playing ugly Yahoo tricks.

Factory windows are always broken.
Other windows are let alone.
No one throws through the chapel-window
The bitter, snarling, derisive stone.

Factory windows are always broken.
Something or other is going wrong.
Something is rotten — I think, in Denmark.
End of the factory-window song.

TO MARY PICKFORD

Moving-picture Actress

(On hearing she was leaving the moving-pictures for the stage.)

Mary Pickford, doll divine,
Year by year, and every day
At the moving-picture play,
You have been my valentine.

Once a free-limbed page in hose,
Baby-Rosalind in flower,
Cloakless, shrinking, in that hour
How our reverent passion rose,
How our fine desire you won.
Kitchen-wench another day,
Shapeless, wooden every way.
Next, a fairy from the sun.

Once you walked a grown-up strand
Fish-wife siren, full of lure,

Snaring with devices sure
Lads who murdered on the sand.
But on most days just a child
Dimpled as no grown-folk are,
Cold of kiss as some north star,
Violet from the valleys wild.
Snared as innocence must be,
Fleeing, prisoned, chained, half-dead —
At the end of tortures dread
Roaring cowboys set you free.

Fly, O song, to her to-day,
Like a cowboy cross the land.
Snatch her from Belasco's hand
And that prison called Broadway.

All the village swains await
One dear lily-girl demure,
Saucy, dancing, cold and pure,
Elf who must return in state.

BLANCHE SWEET

Moving-picture Actress

(After seeing the reel called "Oil and Water.")

Beauty has a throne-room
In our humorous town,
Spoiling its hob-goblins,
Laughing shadows down.
Rank musicians torture
Ragtime ballads vile,
But we walk serenely
Down the odorous aisle.
We forgive the squalor
And the boom and squeal
For the Great Queen flashes
From the moving reel.

Just a prim blonde stranger
In her early day,
Hiding brilliant weapons,
Too averse to play,

Then she burst upon us
Dancing through the night.
Oh, her maiden radiance,
Veils and roses white.
With new powers, yet cautious,
Not too smart or skilled,
That first flash of dancing
Wrought the thing she willed: —
Mobs of us made noble
By her strong desire,
By her white, uplifting,
Royal romance-fire.

Though the tin piano
Snarls its tango rude,
Though the chairs are shaky
And the dramas crude,
Solemn are her motions,
Stately are her wiles,
Filling oafs with wisdom,
Saving souls with smiles;
'Mid the restless actors
She is rich and slow.
She will stand like marble,
She will pause and glow,

Though the film is twitching,
Keep a peaceful reign,
Ruler of her passion,
Ruler of our pain!

SUNSHINE

FOR A VERY LITTLE GIRL, NOT A YEAR OLD.
CATHARINE FRAZEE WAKEFIELD.

The sun gives not directly
  The coal, the diamond crown;
Not in a special basket
  Are these from Heaven let down.

The sun gives not directly
  The plough, man's iron friend;
Not by a path or stairway
  Do tools from Heaven descend.

Yet sunshine fashions all things
  That cut or burn or fly;
And corn that seems upon the earth
  Is made in the hot sky.

The gravel of the roadbed,
  The metal of the gun,
The engine of the airship
  Trace somehow from the sun.

And so your soul, my lady --
   (Mere sunshine, nothing more) —
Prepares me the contraptions
   I work with or adore.

Within me cornfields rustle,
   Niagaras roar their way,
Vast thunderstorms and rainbows
   Are in my thought to-day.

Ten thousand anvils sound there
   By forges flaming white,
And many books I read there,
   And many books I write;

And freedom's bells are ringing,
   And bird-choirs chant and fly —
The whole world works in me to-day
   And all the shining sky,

Because of one small lady
   Whose smile is my chief sun.
She gives not any gift to me
   Yet all gifts, giving one. . . .
                     Amen.

AN APOLOGY FOR THE BOTTLE VOLCANIC

Sometimes I dip my pen and find the bottle
   full of fire,
The salamanders flying forth I cannot but
   admire.
It's Etna, or Vesuvius, if those big things
   were small,
And then 'tis but itself again, and does not
   smoke at all.
And so my blood grows cold. I say, "The
   bottle held but ink,
And, if you thought it otherwise, the worser
   for your think."
And then, just as I throw my scribbled
   paper on the floor,
The bottle says, "Fe, fi, fo, fum," and steams
   and shouts some more.
O sad deceiving ink, as bad as liquor in its
   way —
All demons of a bottle size have pranced
   from you to-day,

I

And seized my pen for hobby-horse as
     witches ride a broom,
And left a trail of brimstone words and
     blots and gobs of gloom.
And yet when I am extra good and say my
     prayers at night,
And mind my ma, and do the chores, and
     speak to folks polite,
My bottle spreads a rainbow-mist, and from
     the vapor fine
Ten thousand troops from fairyland come
     riding in a line.
I've seen them on their chargers race around
     my study chair,
They opened wide the window and rode
     forth upon the air.
The army widened as it went, and into
     myriads grew,
O how the lances shimmered, how the
     silvery trumpets blew !

WHEN GASSY THOMPSON STRUCK IT RICH

He paid a Swede twelve bits an hour
Just to invent a fancy style
To spread the celebration paint
So it would show at least a mile.

Some things they did I will not tell.
They're not quite proper for a rhyme.
But I WILL say Yim Yonson Swede
Did sure invent a sunflower time.

One thing they did that I can tell
And not offend the ladies here: —
They took a goat to Simp's Saloon
And made it take a bath in beer.

That ENTERprise took MANagement.
They broke a wash-tub in the fray.
But mister goat was bathed all right
And bar-keep Simp was, too, they say.

They wore girls' pink straw hats to church
And clucked like hens.   They surely did.
They bought two нotel frying pans
And in them down the mountain slid.

They went to Denver in good clothes,
And kept Burt's grill-room wide awake,
And cut about like jumping-jacks,
And ordered seven-dollar steak.

They had the waiters whirling round
Just sweeping up the smear and smash.
They tried to buy the State-house flag.
They showed the Janitor the cash.

And old Dan Tucker on a toot,
Or John Paul Jones before the breeze,
Or Indians eating fat fried dog,
Were not as happy babes as these.

One morn, in hills near Cripple-creek
With cheerful swears the two awoke.
The Swede had twenty cents, all right.
But Gassy Thompson was clean broke.

RHYMES FOR GLORIANA

I. The Doll upon the Topmost Bough

This doll upon the topmost bough,
This playmate-gift, in Christmas dress,
Was taken down and brought to me
One sleety night most comfortless.

Her hair was gold, her dolly-sash
Was gray brocade, most good to see.
The dear toy laughed, and I forgot
The ill the new year promised me.

II. On suddenly receiving a Curl Long Refused

Oh, saucy gold circle of fairyland silk —
Impudent, intimate, delicate treasure :
A noose for my heart and a ring for my
      finger : —
Here in my study you sing me a measure.

Whimsy and song in my little gray study !
Words out of wonderland, praising her
      fineness,

Touched with her pulsating, delicate
    laughter,
Saying, "The girl is all daring and kindness!"

Saying, "Her soul is all feminine gameness,
Trusting her insights, ardent for living;
She would be weeping with me and be
    laughing,
A thoroughbred, joyous receiving and
    giving!"

III. ON RECEIVING ONE OF GLORIANA'S LETTERS

Your pen needs but a ruffle
To be Pavlova whirling.
It surely is a scalawag
A-scamping down the page.
A pretty little May-wind
The morning buds uncurling.
And then the white sweet Russian,
The dancer of the age.

Your pen's the Queen of Sheba,
Such serious questions bringing,
That merry rascal Solomon
Would show a sober face: —

And then again Pavlova
To set our spirits singing,
The snowy-swan bacchante
All glamour, glee and grace.

IV. In Praise of Gloriana's Remarkable Golden Hair

The gleaming head of one fine friend
Is bent above my little song,
So through the treasure-pits of Heaven
In fancy's shoes, I march along.

I wander, seek and peer and ponder
In Splendor's last ensnaring lair —
'Mid burnished harps and burnished crowns
Where noble chariots gleam and flare :

Amid the spirit-coins and gems,
The plates and cups and helms of fire —
The gorgeous-treasure-pits of Heaven —
Where angel-misers slake desire !

O endless treasure-pits of gold
Where silly angel-men make mirth —
I think that I am there this hour,
Though walking in the ways of earth !

FOURTH SECTION

TWENTY POEMS IN WHICH THE MOON IS THE PRINCIPAL FIGURE OF SPEECH

ONCE MORE — TO GLORIANA

Girl with the burning golden eyes,
And red-bird song, and snowy throat:
I bring you gold and silver moons
And diamond stars, and mists that float.
I bring you moons and snowy clouds,
I bring you prairie skies to-night
To feebly praise your golden eyes
And red-bird song, and throat so white.

I. FAIRY-TALES FOR THE CHILDREN

I. *Euclid*

Old Euclid drew a circle
On a sand-beach long ago.
He bounded and enclosed it
With angles thus and so.
His set of solemn greybeards
Nodded and argued much
Of arc and of circumference,
Diameter and such.

A silent child stood by them
From morning until noon
Because they drew such charming
Round pictures of the moon.

II. THE HAUGHTY SNAIL-KING

(What Uncle William told the Children)

Twelve snails went walking after night.
They'd creep an inch or so,
Then stop and bug their eyes
And blow.
Some folks . . . are . . . deadly . . . slow.
Twelve snails went walking yestereve,
Led by their fat old king.
They were so dull their princeling had
No sceptre, robe or ring —
Only a paper cap to wear
When nightly journeying.

This king-snail said: "I feel a thought
Within. . . .   It blossoms soon. . . .
O little courtiers of mine, . . .
I crave a pretty boon. . . .
Oh, yes . . . (High thoughts with effort come

And well-bred snails are ALMOST dumb.)
"I wish I had a yellow crown
As glistering . . . as . . . the moon."

III. WHAT THE RATTLESNAKE SAID

The moon's a little prairie-dog.
He shivers through the night.
He sits upon his hill and cries
For fear that *I* will bite.

The sun's a broncho.   He's afraid
Like every other thing,
And trembles, morning, noon and night,
Lest *I* should spring, and sting.

IV. THE MOON'S THE NORTH WIND'S COOKY

(What the Little Girl Said)

The Moon's the North Wind's cooky.
He bites it, day by day,
Until there's but a rim of scraps
That crumble all away.

The South Wind is a baker.
He kneads clouds in his den,

And bakes a crisp new moon *that . . . greedy*
North . . . Wind . . . eats . . . again !

V. DRYING THEIR WINGS

(*What the Carpenter Said*)

The moon's a cottage with a door.
Some folks can see it plain.
Look, you may catch a glint of light,
A sparkle through the pane,
Showing the place is brighter still
Within, though bright without.
There, at a cosy open fire
Strange babes are grouped about.
The children of the wind and tide —
The urchins of the sky,
Drying their wings from storms and things
So they again can fly.

VI. WHAT THE GRAY-WINGED FAIRY SAID

The moon's a gong, hung in the wild,
Whose song the fays hold dear.
Of course you do not hear it, child.
It takes a FAIRY ear.

The full moon is a splendid gong
That beats as night grows still.
It sounds above the evening song
Of dove or whippoorwill.

VII. Yet Gentle will the Griffin Be

(*What Grandpa told the Children*)

The moon?   It is a griffin's egg,
Hatching to-morrow night.
And how the little boys will watch
With shouting and delight
To see him break the shell and stretch
And creep across the sky.
The boys will laugh.   The little girls,
I fear, may hide and cry.
Yet gentle will the griffin be,
Most decorous and fat,
And walk up to the milky way
And lap it like a cat.

Second Section of the Moon Series

THE MOON IS A MIRROR

I. Prologue. A Sense of Humor

No man should stand before the moon
To make sweet song thereon,
With dandified importance,
His sense of humor gone.

Nay, let us don the motley cap,
The jester's chastened mien,
If we would woo that looking-glass
And see what should be seen.

O mirror on fair Heaven's wall,
We find there what we bring.
So, let us smile in honest part
And deck our souls and sing.

Yea, by the chastened jest alone
Will ghosts and terrors pass,
And fays, or suchlike friendly things,
Throw kisses through the glass.

II. On the Garden-wall

Oh, once I walked a garden
In dreams. 'Twas yellow grass.
And many orange-trees grew there
In sand as white as glass.
The curving, wide wall-border
Was marble, like the snow.
I walked that wall a fairy-prince
And, pacing quaint and slow,
Beside me were my pages,
Two giant, friendly birds.
Half-swan they were, half peacock.
They spake in courtier-words.
Their inner wings a chariot,
Their outer wings for flight,
They lifted me from dreamland.
We bade those trees good-night.
Swiftly above the stars we rode.
I looked below me soon.
The white-walled garden I had ruled
Was one lone flower — the moon.

K

III. Written for a Musician

Hungry for music with a desperate hunger
I prowled abroad, I threaded through the
　　town;
The evening crowd was clamoring and
　　drinking,
Vulgar and pitiful — my heart bowed
　　down —
Till I remembered duller hours made noble
By strangers clad in some surprising grace.
Wait, wait, my soul, your music comes ere
　　midnight
Appearing in some unexpected place
With quivering lips, and gleaming, moonlit
　　face.

IV. The Moon is a Painter

He coveted her portrait.
He toiled as she grew gay.
She loved to see him labor
In that devoted way.

And in the end it pleased her,
But bowed him more with care.

Her rose-smile showed so plainly,
Her soul-smile was not there.

That night he groped without a lamp
To find a cloak, a book,
And on the vexing portrait
By moonrise chanced to look.

The color-scheme was out of key,
The maiden rose-smile faint,
But through the blessed darkness
She gleamed, his friendly saint.

The comrade, white, immortal,
His bride, and more than bride —
The citizen, the sage of mind,
For whom he lived and died.

V. The Encyclopædia

"If I could set the moon upon
This table," said my friend,
"Among the standard poets
And brouchures without end,
And noble prints of old Japan,
How empty they would seem,

By that encyclopædia
Of whim and glittering dream."

VI. What the Miner in the Desert Said

The moon's a brass-hooped water-keg,
A wondrous water-feast.
If I could climb the ridge and drink
And give drink to my beast;
If I could drain that keg, the flies
Would not be biting so,
My burning feet be spry again,
My mule no longer slow.
And I could rise and dig for ore,
And reach my fatherland,
And not be food for ants and hawks
And perish in the sand.

VII. What the Coal-heaver Said

The moon's an open furnace door
Where all can see the blast,
We shovel in our blackest griefs,
Upon that grate are cast
Our aching burdens, loves and fears
And underneath them wait

Paper and tar and pitch and pine
Called strife and blood and hate.

Out of it all there comes a flame,
A splendid widening light.
Sorrow is turned to mystery
 And Death into delight.

VIII. What the Moon Saw

Two statesmen met by moonlight.
Their ease was partly feigned.
They glanced about the prairie.
Their faces were constrained.
In various ways aforetime
They had misled the state,
Yet did it so politely
Their henchmen thought them great.
They sat beneath a hedge and spake
No word, but had a smoke.
A satchel passed from hand to hand.
Next day, the deadlock broke.

IX. What Semiramis Said

The moon's a steaming chalice
  Of honey and venom-wine.
A little of it sipped by night
  Makes the long hours divine.
But oh, my reckless lovers,
  They drain the cup and wail,
Die at my feet with shaking limbs
  And tender lips all pale.
Above them in the sky it bends
  Empty and gray and dread.
To-morrow night 'tis full again,
  Golden, and foaming red.

X. What the Ghost of the Gambler Said

Where now the huts are empty,
Where never a camp-fire glows,
In an abandoned cañon,
A Gambler's Ghost arose.
He muttered there, "The moon's a sack
Of dust." His voice rose thin:
"I wish I knew the miner-man.
I'd play, and play to win.
In every game in Cripple-creek

Of old, when stakes were high,
I held my own.   Now I would play
For that sack in the sky.
The sport would not be ended there.
'Twould rather be begun.
I'd bet my moon against his stars,
And gamble for the sun."

XI. THE SPICE-TREE

This is the song
The spice-tree sings:
"Hunger and fire,
Hunger and fire,
Sky-born Beauty —
Spice of desire,"
Under the spice-tree
Watch and wait,
Burning maidens
And lads that mate.

The spice-tree spreads
And its boughs come down
Shadowing village and farm and town.
And none can see
But the pure of heart

The great green leaves
And the boughs descending,
And hear the song that is never ending.

The deep roots whisper,
The branches say : —
"Love to-morrow,
And love to-day,
And till Heaven's day,
And till Heaven's day."

The moon is a bird's nest in its branches,
The moon is hung in its topmost spaces.
And there, to-night, two doves play house
While lovers watch with uplifted faces.
Two doves go home
To their nest, the moon.
It is woven of twigs of broken light,
With threads of scarlet and threads of gray
And a lining of down for silk delight.
To their Eden, the moon, fly home our doves,
Up through the boughs of the great spice-
      tree ; —
And one is the kiss I took from you,
And one is the kiss you gave to me.

XII. The Scissors-grinder

(*What the Tramp Said*)

The old man had his box and wheel
For grinding knives and shears.
No doubt his bell in village streets
Was joy to children's ears.
And I bethought me of my youth
When such men came around,
And times I asked them in, quite sure
The scissors should be ground.
The old man turned and spoke to me,
His face at last in view.
And then I thought those curious eyes
Were eyes that once I knew.

"The moon is but an emery-wheel
To whet the sword of God,"
He said. "And here beside my fire
I stretch upon the sod
Each night, and dream, and watch the stars
And watch the ghost-clouds go.
And see that sword of God in Heaven
A-waving to and fro.

I see that sword each century, friend.
It means the world-war comes
With all its bloody, wicked chiefs
And hate-inflaming drums.
Men talk of peace, but I have seen
That emery-wheel turn round.
The voice of Abel cries again
To God from out the ground.
The ditches must flow red, the plague
Go stark and screaming by
Each time that sword of God takes edge
Within the midnight sky.
And those that scorned their brothers here
And sowed a wind of shame
Will reap the whirlwind as of old
And face relentless flame."

And thus the scissors-grinder spoke,
His face at last in view.
And there beside the railroad bridge
I saw the wandering Jew.

XIII. My Lady in her White Silk Shawl

My lady in her white silk shawl
  Is like a lily dim,
Within the twilight of the room
  Enthroned and kind and prim.

My lady ! Pale gold is her hair.
  Until she smiles her face
Is pale with far Hellenic moods,
  With thoughts that find no place

In our harsh village of the West
  Wherein she lives of late,
She's distant as far-hidden stars,
  And cold — (almost !) — as fate.

But when she smiles she's here again
  Rosy with comrade-cheer,
A Puritan Bacchante made
  To laugh around the year.

The merry gentle moon herself,
  Heart-stirring too, like her,
Wakening wild and innocent love
  In every worshipper.

XIV. Aladdin and the Jinn

"Bring me soft song," said Aladdin.
"This tailor-shop sings not at all.
Chant me a word of the twilight,
Of roses that mourn in the fall.
Bring me a song like hashish
That will comfort the stale and the sad,
For I would be mending my spirit,
Forgetting these days that are bad,
Forgetting companions too shallow,
Their quarrels and arguments thin,
Forgetting the shouting Muezzin:" —
"I am your slave," said the Jinn.

"Bring me old wines," said Aladdin.
"I have been a starved pauper too long.
Serve them in vessels of jade and of shell,
Serve them with fruit and with song: —
Wines of pre-Adamite Sultans
Digged from beneath the black seas: —
New-gathered dew from the heavens
Dripped down from Heaven's sweet trees,
Cups from the angels' pale tables
That will make me both handsome and wise,

For I have beheld her, the princess,
Firelight and starlight her eyes.
Pauper I am, I would woo her.
And — let me drink wine, to begin,
Though the Koran expressly forbids it."
"I AM YOUR SLAVE," said the Jinn.

"Plan me a dome," said Aladdin,
"That is drawn like the dawn of the MOON,
When the sphere seems to rest on the
    mountains,
Half-hidden, yet full-risen soon."
"Build me a dome," said Aladdin,
" That shall cause all young lovers to sigh,
The fullness of life and of beauty,
Peace beyond peace to the eye —
A palace of foam and of opal,
Pure moonlight without and within,
Where I may enthrone my sweet lady."
"I AM YOUR SLAVE," said the Jinn.

XV. The Strength of the Lonely

(What the Mendicant Said)

The moon's a monk, unmated,
Who walks his cell, the sky.
His strength is that of heaven-vowed men
Who all life's flames defy.

They turn to stars or shadows,
They go like snow or dew —
Leaving behind no sorrow —
Only the arching blue.

WAR. SEPTEMBER 1, 1914
INTENDED TO BE READ ALOUD

I. ABRAHAM LINCOLN WALKS AT MIDNIGHT

(In Springfield, Illinois)

It is portentous, and a thing of state
That here at midnight, in our little town
A mourning figure walks, and will not rest,
Near the old court-house pacing up and
    down,

Or by his homestead, or in shadowed yards
He lingers where his children used to play,
Or through the market, on the well-worn
    stones
He stalks until the dawn-stars burn away.

A bronzed, lank man! His suit of ancient
    black,
A famous high top-hat and plain worn
    shawl
Make him the quaint great figure that men
    love,
The prairie-lawyer, master of us all.

He cannot sleep upon his hillside now.
He is among us : — as in times before !
And we who toss and lie awake for long
Breathe deep, and start, to see him pass the
    door.

His head is bowed.   He thinks on men and
    kings.
Yea, when the sick world cries, how can he
    sleep ?
Too many peasants fight, they know not why,
Too many homesteads in black terror weep.

The sins of all the war-lords burn his heart.
He sees the dreadnaughts scouring every
    main.
He carries on his shawl-wrapped shoulders
    now
The bitterness, the folly and the pain.

He cannot rest until a spirit-dawn
Shall come ; — the shining hope of Europe
    free :
The league of sober folk, the Workers'
    Earth,

Bringing long peace to Cornland, Alp and
    Sea.

It breaks his heart that kings must murder
    still,
That all his hours of travail here for men
Seem yet in vain.   And who will bring white
    peace
That he may sleep upon his hill again?

II. A CURSE FOR KINGS

A curse upon each king who leads his
 state,
No matter what his plea, to this foul
 game,
And may it end his wicked dynasty,
And may he die in exile and black shame.

If there is vengeance in the Heaven of
 Heavens,
What punishment could Heaven devise for
 these
Who fill the rivers of the world with dead,
And turn their murderers loose on all the
 seas !

Put back the clock of time a thousand
 years,
And make our Europe, once the world's
 proud Queen,
A shrieking strumpet, furious fratricide,
Eater of entrails, wallowing obscene

In pits where millions foam and rave and
 bark,
Mad dogs and idiots, thrice drunk with
 strife;
While Science towers above; — a witch, red-
 winged:
Science we looked to for the light of life.

Curse me the men who make and sell iron
 ships,
Who walk the floor in thought, that they
 may find
Each powder prompt, each steel with fearful edge,
Each deadliest device against mankind.

Curse me the sleek lords with their plumes
 and spurs,
May Heaven give their land to peasant
 spades,
Give them the brand of Cain, for their pride's
 sake,
And felon's stripes for medals and for
 braids.

Curse me the fiddling, twiddling diplomats,
Haggling here, plotting and hatching there,
Who make the kind world but their game of
    cards,
Till millions die at turning of a hair.

What punishment will Heaven devise for
    these
Who win by others' sweat and hardihood,
Who make men into stinking vultures' meat,
Saying to evil still "Be thou my good"?

Ah, he who starts a million souls toward
    death
Should burn in utmost hell a million years!
— Mothers of men go on the destined wrack
To give them life, with anguish and with
    tears : —

Are all those childbed sorrows sneered away?
Yea, fools laugh at the humble christenings,
And cradle-joys are mocked of the fat
    lords :
These mothers' sons made dead men for the
    Kings !

All in the name of this or that grim flag,
No angel-flags in all the rag-array —
Banners the demons love, and all Hell sings
And plays wild harps.   Those flags march
    forth to-day !

III. WHO KNOWS ?

They say one king is mad. Perhaps. Who
    knows ?
They say one king is doddering and grey.
They say one king is slack and sick of mind,
A puppet for hid strings that twitch and
    play.

Is Europe then to be their sprawling-place ?
Their mad-house, till it turns the wide
    world's bane ?
Their place of maudlin, slavering conference
Till every far-off farmstead goes insane ?

IV. TO BUDDHA

Awake again in Asia, Lord of Peace,
Awake and preach, for her far swordsmen
      rise.
And would they sheathe the sword before
      you, friend,
Or scorn your way, while looking in your
      eyes ?

Good comrade and philosopher and prince,
Thoughtful and thoroughbred and strong
      and kind,
Dare they to move against your pride benign,
Lord of the Law, high chieftain of the mind ?
      *   *   *   *   *
But what can Europe say, when in your name
The throats are cut, the lotus-ponds turn
      red ?
And what can Europe say, when with a laugh
Old Asia heaps her hecatombs of dead ?

V. THE UNPARDONABLE SIN

This is the sin against the Holy Ghost : —
To speak of bloody power as right divine,
And call on God to guard each vile chief's
     house,
And for such chiefs, turn men to wolves and
     swine : —

To go forth killing in White Mercy's name,
Making the trenches stink with spattered
     brains,
Tearing the nerves and arteries apart,
Sowing with flesh the unreaped golden
     plains.

In any Church's name, to sack fair towns,
And turn each home into a screaming sty,
To make the little children fugitive,
And have their mothers for a quick death
     cry, —

This is the sin against the Holy Ghost :
This is the sin no purging can atone : —
To send forth rapine in the name of
   Christ : —
To set the face, and make the heart a
   stone.

VI. ABOVE THE BATTLE'S FRONT

St. Francis, Buddha, Tolstoi, and St. John —
Friends, if you four, as pilgrims, hand in
        hand,
Returned, the hate of earth once more to
        dare,
And walked upon the water and the land,

If you, with words celestial, stopped these
        kings
For sober conclave, ere their battle great,
Would they for one deep instant then
        discern
Their crime, their heart-rot, and their fiend's
        estate?

If you should float above the battle's
        front,
Pillars of cloud, of fire that does not slay,
Bearing a fifth within your regal train,
The Son of David in his strange array —

If, in his majesty, he towered toward Heaven,
Would they have hearts to see or under-
    stand ?
. . . Nay, for he hovers there to-night we
    know,
Thorn-crowned above the water and the
    land.

VII. EPILOGUE

Under the Blessing of your Psyche Wings

Though I have found you like a snow-drop
　　pale,
On sunny days have found you weak and
　　still,
Though I have often held your girlish head
Drooped on my shoulder, faint from little
　　ill : —

Under the blessing of your Psyche-wings
I hide to-night like one small broken bird,
So soothed I half-forget the world gone
　　mad : —
And all the winds of war are now unheard.

My heaven-doubting pennons feel your
　　hands
With touch most delicate so circling round,
That for an hour I dream that God is good.
And in your shadow, Mercy's ways abound.

I thought myself the guard of your frail
  state,
And yet I come to-night a helpless guest,
Hiding beneath your giant Psyche-wings,
Against the pallor of your wondrous breast.

NEW Poems and Plays published by
The Macmillan Company.

RABINDRANATH TAGORE'S NEW DRAMA

The King of the Dark Chamber

By

RABINDRANATH TAGORE

Nobel Prizeman in Literature, 1913; Author of "Gitan-
gali," "The Gardener," "The Crescent Moon,"
"Sadhana," "Chitra," "The Post-Office," etc. Cloth
12 mo, $1.25 *net*.

"The real poetical imagination of it is unchangeable;
the allegory, subtle and profound and yet simple, is cast
into the form of a dramatic narrative, which moves with
unconventional freedom to a finely impressive climax; and
the reader, who began in idle curiosity, finds his intelligence
more and more engaged until, when he turns the last page,
he has the feeling of one who has been moving in worlds
not realized, and communing with great if mysterious
presences."

The London Globe.

PUBLISHED BY

THE MACMILLAN COMPANY

Publishers   64-66 Fifth Avenue   New York

You and I

By HARRIET MONROE

Cloth, 12mo, $1.25 net

In this book is brought together some of Miss Monroe's best work. As the editor of *Poetry: A Magazine of Verse*, wherein occasionally compositions of her own have appeared, and as a contributor to the better magazines, Miss Monroe has endeared herself to a large audience of discriminating people. A distinguishing feature of the collection is that it is notably representative of current ideas and sentiments, and pleasingly varied in theme. The author's subjects are chosen from the Panama Canal, the Titantic disaster, the turbine, the telephone, State Street, Chicago, and other modern phases or factors of life. There is also a group of love poems.

Borderlands and Thoroughfares

By WILFRID WILSON GIBSON

Author of " Daily Bread," " Fires," " Womenkind," etc.

Cloth, 12mo, $1.25 net

With the publication of *Daily Bread* Mr. Gibson was hailed as a new poet of the people. *Fires*, his later volume, confirmed the impression that here was a man whose writing was close to real life, a man in whom were combined a sympathy and appreciation of humankind with a rare lyrical genius. This present book continues the work which Mr. Gibson can do so well. In it are brought together three plays and a number of short lyrics which reveal again his very decided talent. It is a collection which should indeed gratify those students of modern verse who are looking to such men as Gibson and Masefield for permanent and representative contributions to literature.

THE MACMILLAN COMPANY

Publishers   64-66 Fifth Avenue   New York

Earth Triumphant and Other Tales in Verse

By CONRAD AIKEN

Cloth, 12mo, $1.25 net

Conrad Aiken is one of the first American writers to choose to tell his stories in verse. Helston, Masefield, and other Europeans have been doing it with marked success, but hitherto this country has had no notable representative in this line of endeavor. Though Mr. Aiken has been writing for a number of years, *Earth Triumphant and Other Tales in Verse* is his first published book. In it are contained, in addition to the several narratives of modern life, a number of shorter lyrics. It is a volume distinguished by originality and power.

Van Zorn : A Comedy in Three Acts

By EDWIN A. ROBINSON

Cloth, 12mo, $1.25 net

This play makes delightful reading and introduces in the person of its author a playwright of considerable promise. Mr. Robinson tells an interesting story, one which by a clever arrangement of incident and skillful characterization arouses strongly the reader's curiosity and keeps it unsatisfied to the end. The dialogue is bright and the construction of the plot shows the work of one well versed in the technique of the drama.

THE MACMILLAN COMPANY

Publishers   64-66 Fifth Avenue   New York

Plaster Saints

BY ISRAEL ZANGWILL. Cloth, 12mo. $1.25 net.

A new play of deep social significance.

The Melting Pot

BY ISRAEL ZANGWILL. Revised edition. Cloth, 12mo.

This is a revised edition of what is perhaps Mr. Zangwill's most popular play. Numerous changes have been made in the text, which has been considerably lengthened thereby. The appeal of the drama to the readers of this country is particularly strong, in that it deals with that great social process by which all nationalities are blended together for the making of the real American.

Sword Blades and Poppy Seed

BY AMY LOWELL, Author of "A Dome of Many-Coloured Glass." Boards, 12mo. $1.25 net.

Of the poets who to-day are doing the interesting and original work, there is no more striking and unique figure than Amy Lowell. The foremost American member of the "Imagists"—a group of poets that includes William Butler Yeats, Ezra Pound, Ford Madox Hueffer—she has won wide recognition for her writing in new and free forms of poetical expression. Miss Lowell's present volume of poems, "Sword Blades and Poppy Seed," is an unusual book. It contains much perhaps that will arouse criticism, but it is a new note in American poetry. Miss Lowell has broken away from academic traditions and written, out of her own time, real singing poetry, free, full of new effects and subtleties.

PUBLISHED BY

THE MACMILLAN COMPANY

Publishers   64-66 Fifth Avenue   **New York**

A LIST OF PLAYS

PUBLISHED BY

THE MACMILLAN COMPANY

Publishers   64–66 Fifth Avenue   New York